First World War
and Army of Occupation
War Diary
France, Belgium and Germany

24 DIVISION
72 Infantry Brigade,
Brigade Trench Mortar Battery
3 February 1918 - 31 January 1919

WO95/2215/3

The Naval & Military Press Ltd
www.nmarchive.com
Published in association with The National Archives

Published by

The Naval & Military Press Ltd

Unit 10 Ridgewood Industrial Park,

Uckfield, East Sussex,

TN22 5QE England

Tel: +44 (0) 1825 749494

www.naval-military-press.com

www.nmarchive.com

This diary has been reprinted in facsimile from the original. Any imperfections are inevitably reproduced and the quality may fall short of modern type and cartographic standards.

© **Crown Copyright**
Images reproduced by permission of The National Archives, London, England, 2015.

Contents

Document type	Place/Title	Date From	Date To
Heading	WO95/2215/3		
Heading	72nd Trench Moratr Bty Feb 1918-Jan 1919		
War Diary	In The Field	03/02/1918	20/02/1918
War Diary	Field	20/02/1918	27/02/1918
Heading	1st to 30th June 1918 72nd Light Trench Mortar Battery.		
War Diary	Combat Trench	07/06/1918	09/06/1918
War Diary	Cite St Pierre	10/06/1918	29/06/1918
Heading	War Diary Of 72nd Light Trench Mortar Battery. From July 1st. To July 31st 1918.		
War Diary		01/07/1918	02/07/1918
War Diary	Sains-En-Gohelle	03/07/1918	07/07/1918
War Diary	Combat	07/07/1918	23/07/1918
War Diary	Combat Tr.	25/07/1918	31/07/1918
Heading	War Diary Of 72nd L. Trench Mortar Battery 1st August to 31st August 1918. Volume IV.		
War Diary		02/08/1918	31/08/1918
Heading	War Diary 72nd T.M. Batty. September 1918		
War Diary		01/09/1918	30/09/1918
Heading	War Diary 72nd Light Trench Mortar Batty. October 1918		
War Diary		01/10/1918	31/10/1918
War Diary	Period	07/10/1918	15/10/1918
War Diary	Haussy	16/10/1918	16/10/1918
War Diary		01/12/1918	31/12/1918
War Diary		01/01/1919	31/01/1919

Woche 22.5.|3

24TH DIVISION
72ND INFY BDE

72ND TRENCH MORATR BTY

FEB 1918 - JAN 1919

24TH DIVISION
72ND INFY BDE

WAR DIARY 42 Trench Mortar Battery
INTELLIGENCE SUMMARY

Army Form C. 2118.

(Erase heading not required.)

Feb. 18 / Jan '19

Place	Date	Hour	Summary of Events and Information	Remarks and references to Appendices
In the field	3/2/18	–	The Battery cooperated in a raid with the Royal West Kent Regt. 24 rounds were fired on enemy's front + support lines + on expected T.M. + machine gun positions.	
	4/2/18	–	Bty replied to "S.O.S" signal, firing 142 rounds on enemy's front line + barbed wire.	
	7/2/18	–	42" T.M. Battery was relieved in the line by 19 A.T.M. Battery + proceeded to HANCOURT.	
	10/2/18	–	1 officer + 15 O.R. were transferred to 17 A T.M. Battery. 7394 Sgt Saunders [& R. West Kent Regt] rejoined this unit from 2nd Army 42. T.M.B.	
	1.2.18		Div: Cavalry Division where he was acting as instructor on Stokes 3" Gun. Three men proceeded on leave (Ptes Shaw, Poole Loveno).	
	4-2-19		42. T.M. Battery relieves the 2nd Div: Bn: Divn: in the line at HARROS STORES. Seven guns were taken over.	
	20-2-19		No 2 + 3 guns were withdrawn from VILLERET LANE, positions were made in VILLE RET and PRIEL WOODS.	

(cont).

WAR DIARY 72" Trench Mortar Batt.y
or
INTELLIGENCE SUMMARY.
(Erase heading not required.)

Army Form C. 2118.

Place	Date	Hour	Summary of Events and Information	Remarks and references to Appendices
Field	20/2/18	—	Casualties 2.O.R. wounded.	
"	20/2/18	—	Sgt Saunders A.1394 and 6346 Pt Ivey proceeded on leave to ENGLAND.	
"	21/2/18	—	16 reinforcements arrived. 5 Royal West Kent Regt, 5, 1st N. Staffs. Regt, 1, 6, 7th Lincolns.	
"	22/2/18	—	17 T.M. Battery took over our positions in SPADE LANE.	
			This gun moved into position at top of VILLERET LANE.	
	24-2-18	—	Ptes 5915 Ogilvie & 8882 Pt Nicholls returned from leave in ENGLAND.	
	24/2/18	—	Presentation of medals at MONTIGNY. 1 N.C.O. & 2 men attended, 6.O.R. benign leave.	
	25/2/18	—	2 guns moved into positions in PRIEL WOODS.	
			No 2 gun withdrew from line into position in VILLERET.	
	26/2/18	—	72. T.M. Battery was relieved in the line by 199th T.M. Battery	
	26/2/18	—	The Battery proceeded to ROISEL.	
	27/2/18	—	72. T.M. Battery proceeded by Train to CORBIE.	
			For month of February, 1098 rounds were fired.	
			Casualties for month, 2.O.R. wounded.	

M.Lucken Capt.
O/C 72. L.T.M. Battery

WAR DIARY.

1st to 30th June 1918

72nd Light Trench Mortar Battery.

WAR DIARY or INTELLIGENCE SUMMARY.

(Erase heading not required.)

Army Form C. 2118.

for June 1918.

Instructions regarding War Diaries and Intelligence Summaries are contained in F. S. Regs., Part II. and the Staff Manual respectively. Title pages will be prepared in manuscript.

Hour, Date, Place	Summary of Events and Information	Remarks and references to Appendices
June 5th COMBAT. TRENCH.	Antiaircraft gun is in position here. This gun fired on a target given by the Infantry. Scale of retaliation is now determined by the commander of the Coy behind whose front the gun is in position.	
June 6th	1 O.R. proceed on special leave to CANADA. He has been struck off the strength of this Unit. 1 O.R was also struck of the strength having been in hospital 7 days. Effective Strength is now 4 + 44. Owing to the prevalent fine weather, roads & trenches are in good condition.	
June 7th	Gun activity was confined to targets given by the Infantry. 2 O.R reinforcement arrived. 2 O.R were posted to complete establishment 4 + 46.	

HEADQUARTERS,
7290
T.M. BATTERY,

WAR DIARY for June 1918
INTELLIGENCE SUMMARY

Army Form C. 2118.

Hour, Date, Place	Summary of Events and Information	Remarks and references to Appendices
June 10. CITÉ ST PIERRE	All reserve guns are in positions in cellars. These cellars are fairly strong & commodious, and allow for large stocks of ammunition, at the same time providing cover for the gun teams. N.C.O.s & few operations they are found to be very satisfactory.	
June 11	Intn. Section relief was carried out, 'A' Section relieving 'B' Section in the line. Relief reached Bty. H.Q.rs (CITÉ ST. PIERRE) at 6 p.m. On relief 'B' Section proceeded to STAINS EN GOHELLE and occupied rest billets.	
June 12.	Every available man fired 5 rounds on camp. Weather still continues fine.	

HEADQUARTERS,
72nd
S.H. BATTERY.

WAR DIARY for June 1918
INTELLIGENCE SUMMARY.
(Erase heading not required.)

Army Form C. 2118.

Instructions regarding War Diaries and Intelligence Summaries are contained in F.S. Regs., Part II. and the Staff Manual respectively. Title pages will be prepared in manuscript.

Hour, Date, Place	Summary of Events and Information	Remarks and references to Appendices
June 15th	1.O.R. was admitted to Field Ambulance suffering from an epidemic which is very prevalent in the Brigade. It is very infectious	
June 16. 1am – 1.15 am	4 guns bombarded enemy front line & C.T's in conjunction with the artillery, in connection with a raid by the 6th R.W. Kent Rgt.	
June 17.	Inter Battery relief was carried out, 'B' Section relieving 'A' Section in the line. Owing to hostility, relief was postponed until 11 pm. On relief 'A' Section marched to SAINS EN GOHELLE, arriving there at 1.45 m on June 18th	
June 18.	Heavy downfall of rain, which has not.	

HEADQUARTERS,
T20
T.M. Battery

WAR DIARY for June 1918
or
INTELLIGENCE SUMMARY.

Army Form C. 2118.

(Erase heading not required.)

Instructions regarding War Diaries and Intelligence
Summaries are contained in F. S. Regs., Part II.
and the Staff Manual respectively. Title pages
will be prepared in manuscript.

Hour, Date, Place	Summary of Events and Information	Remarks and references to Appendices
June 18.	Affected the roads to any great extent. 6. O.R. were returned to their Battalions. 6. O.R. reinforcements arrived. Effective strength of Unit 4 on or 45. 1 O.R. was posted in or 6 complete war establishment 4-46.	
June 19th	1. O.R. admitted to hospital suffering from PYREXIA. Up to the present 2 cases only have been reported in this Unit. The necessary precautions as outlined in 2w Brusd: letter are being taken.	
June 20.	Numbers of men in each billet were reduced. Houses are occupied as billets but as ranks are recommended to keep in the open air much as possible.	

HEADQUARTERS,
7th ?? BATTERY.

WAR DIARY for June 1918
or
INTELLIGENCE SUMMARY.
(Erase heading not required.)

Army Form C. 2118.

Instructions regarding War Diaries and Intelligence
Summaries are contained in F. S. Regs., Part II.
and the Staff Manual respectively. Title pages
will be prepared in manuscript.

Hour, Date, Place	Summary of Events and Information	Remarks and references to Appendices
June 21st CITE ST PIERRE	Two gun positions have been chosen in Celeans in rear. Work was commenced on these positions.	
June 23rd	2nd LT. E. GIBBS was admitted to hospital. 2 O.R. were admitted to hospital with PYREXIA. Inter Section relief was carried out. 'A' Section relieving 'B' Section in the line. No parties cannot reach CITE ST PIERRE in daylight, owing to visibility, the relief was not effected until 12 midnight. On relief 'B' Section proceeded to SAINS EN GOHELLE.	
June 25. Q June 26	2nd LT. A.C. NILSON and 2 O.R. of this unit were admitted to hospital with PYREXIA.	

(9 29 6) W 2791 100,000 8/14 H W V Forms/C. 2118/11.

HEADQUARTERS, 72ND T.M. BATTERY.

Army Form C. 2118.

WAR DIARY for June 1918
or
INTELLIGENCE SUMMARY.
(Erase heading not required.)

Hour, Date, Place	Summary of Events and Information	Remarks and references to Appendices
June 26.	Effective Strength of this Unit is 9 off & 146 O.R. PYREXIA cases are returned on the strength as if not incapable that all cases will return to duty in the course of 10 days.	
June 27.	Condition of roads & trenches is good, as the hot weather still continues. The question of reinforcing all cellars used as gun positions with concrete is being commenced.	
June 29. 11.30 pm	"A" Section relief was carried out, "B" Section relieving "A" Section in the line. Relief was completed and "A" Section proceeded to SAINS EN GOHELLE. Weather continues good.	

J. Wyndham Capt.
O/C 72 T.M. Bty.

CONFIDENTIAL.

WAR DIARY.

OF

72nd LIGHT TRENCH MORTAR BATTERY.

FROM JULY 1st. TO JULY 31st

1918.

Army Form C. 2118.

WAR DIARY
or
INTELLIGENCE SUMMARY.
(Erase heading not required.)

WAR DIARY for July 1918.

Instructions regarding War Diaries and Intelligence Summaries are contained in F. S. Regs., Part II. and the Staff Manual respectively. Title pages will be prepared in manuscript.

Hour, Date, Place	Summary of Events and Information	Remarks and references to Appendices
July 1st	On account of continued spell of good weather the roads and trenches are in good condition. The number of Pyrexia cases has greatly diminished, probably on account of precautions taken, no more cases in this Unit are reported today.	W.S.D.
July 2nd	The warm weather still continues. Average activity is reported by two guns in position in support lines. These guns fire on targets given by the infantry.	W.S.D.
July 3rd SAINS EN GOHELLE	"A" Section proceeds to rifle range. Every man fires 5 rounds S.A.A. By continued practice the shooting has become fairly accurate.	W.S.D.

(9 29 6) W 2791 100,000 8/14 H W V   Forms/C. 2118/11.

Army Form C. 2118.

WAR DIARY for July 1918.
or
INTELLIGENCE SUMMARY.
(Erase heading not required.)

Instructions regarding War Diaries and Intelligence Summaries are contained in F. S. Regs., Part II. and the Staff Manual respectively. Title pages will be prepared in manuscript.

Hour, Date, Place	Summary of Events and Information	Remarks and references to Appendices
July 5.	Inter-Section relief took place. 'A' Section relieving	
	'B' Section in the line	
7.30 pm	'B' Section left its rest billets and proceeded	
	to the line.	
12 p.m.	Relief was completed, a slight delay taking	
	place on account of an artillery shoot to	
	destroy hostile T.M's. On relief 'B' Section proc-	
	eeded to the rest billets.	N.S.D.
July 6.	Two cellars are being adapted for use as	
	reserve gun positions.	
	Having been a coal mining and manufacturing	
	district, this locality is well provided with cellars.	
	These cellars are particularly suitable as gun	
	positions after a few alterations have been	
	effected. The wall facing the front has to	

WAR DIARY for July 1916
or
INTELLIGENCE SUMMARY.

(Erase heading not required.)

Army Form C. 2118.

Instructions regarding War Diaries and Intelligence Summaries are contained in F. S. Regs., Part II. and the Staff Manual respectively. Title pages will be prepared in manuscript.

Hour, Date, Place	Summary of Events and Information	Remarks and references to Appendices
July 6.	(cont) be removed, and therefore large quantities of soil. These are placed on top of the cellar to give additional protection from shell fire. The front when removed, allows for extreme range of the gun being used on the inside floor, by cutting away the bricks as secure access may be made for the baseplate. Ammunition is then stocked in the cellar, where the gun team also lives. When registered the gun remains in its position, its team merely awaiting the 'S.O.S.' signal.	M.S.D.
July 7th. COM BQT. 2.15 p.m.	The weather is still good, and therefore the condition of roads and trenches. A retaliation gun is in position here. Firing at 515 yards range, this gun expended 25.	

C. 2118.

Army Form C. 2118.

WAR DIARY for July 1918
or
INTELLIGENCE SUMMARY.
(Erase heading not required.)

Instructions regarding War Diaries and Intelligence Summaries are contained in F. S. Regs., Part II. and the Staff Manual respectively. Title pages will be prepared in manuscript.

Hour, Date, Place	Summary of Events and Information	Remarks and references to Appendices
(cont)		
July 7 - COMBAT	rounds, were so with a crater as target. This took place at the request of the infantry.	
9.30pm CUTOFF	The gun in position fire fired on Enemy C.T at 608 yards range.	W.S.D.
July 8th	2Lt. NILSON, 9" EAST SURREY. Rgt rejoined this Unit from hospital.	
	From CITÉ-ST-LAURENT, Battery Headquarters was moved to CITÉ-ST-PIERRE. Three cellars are now occupied, all being connected by means of a tunnel, and all built of bricks. All three cellars are gas proof and are very strong.	W.S.D.
July 9th	The weather, hitherto fine for this month has suddenly changed. Rain fell throughout the day, but it did not effect either roads or trenches.	

Army Form C. 2118.

WAR DIARY for July 1918
or
INTELLIGENCE SUMMARY.
(Erase heading not required.)

Instructions regarding War Diaries and Intelligence Summaries are contained in F. S. Regs., Part II. and the Staff Manual respectively. Title pages will be prepared in manuscript.

Hour, Date, Place	Summary of Events and Information	Remarks and references to Appendices
	to any great extent.	
July 11th	Rain fell throughout the day.	
8pm.	'B' Section left its rest billets and proceeded to the line to relieve 'A' Section.	W.S.D.
12pm.	Relief was completed, 'A' Section marched to SAINS-EN-GOHELLE.	W.S.D.
July 12th	Continuous rain fell throughout the day. The soil of this district is largely composed of chalk, which allows the rain to filter through, and leaving the roads comparitively dry. As regards climatical conditions the state of the trenches is also good. 1.O.R. was killed in action. The effective strength of this Unit is now 40f - 43.o.R.	

Army Form C. 2118.

WAR DIARY for JULY
or
INTELLIGENCE SUMMARY.
(Erase heading not required.)

Instructions regarding War Diaries and Intelligence Summaries are contained in F. S. Regs., Part II. and the Staff Manual respectively. Title pages will be prepared in manuscript.

Hour, Date, Place	Summary of Events and Information	Remarks and references to Appendices
July 12th (cont)	Application was today made for 3.O.R. to complete our establishment.	N.S.D.
July 13:	Slight rain fell at intervals throughout the day. The work on two cellars in reserve (which are being adapted for use as gun positions) continues. Owing to visibility work cannot proceed in daylight and any alterations have to be done between the hours of 9 p.m. and 5 a.m.	N.S.D.
July 15th	1. O.R. reported for duty with this Unit. He was placed on the attached strength, which now numbers 1 officer and nineteen O.R.	N.S.D.
July 16:	2. O.R. were struck off the strength, 2 reinforcements O.R. also arriving today. Effective strength being 4 OR on OR 44.	

(9 29 6) W 2794 100,000 8/14 H W V   Forms/C. 2118/11.

WAR DIARY for JULY, 1918.
INTELLIGENCE SUMMARY.

(Erase heading not required.)

Army Form C. 2118.

Instructions regarding War Diaries and Intelligence Summaries are contained in F. S. Regs., Part II. and the Staff Manual respectively. Title pages will be prepared in manuscript.

Hour, Date, Place	Summary of Events and Information	Remarks and references to Appendices
July 16 (cont)	2.O.R. were posted to complete establishment.	N.S.D.
July 17.	Inter Section relief was to-day carried out.	
8 p.m.	The relieving party left SAINS EN GOHELLE and proceeded to the line.	
1 a.m.	Relief was completed 'B' Section no relief marching and taking over its rest billets.	
	There is an noticeable improvement in the weather today.	N.S.D.
July 20.	Steps have been taken to ensure salvage work as outlined in Divisional letter being complied with. Empty ammunition boxes etc are being returned, as also are all fuse tins.	N.S.D.

WAR DIARY for JULY 1918.
or
INTELLIGENCE SUMMARY.

Army Form C. 2118.

Hour, Date, Place	Summary of Events and Information	Remarks and references to Appendices
July 21st	CAPT. C.H.S. WYNDHAM, M.C. proceeded to ENGLAND en route for AMERICA. LT. R.A. WALKER, FR.W. KENT RGT was appointed to, and joined this Unit as from today. 2/LT H.S. DAINTREE proceeded on leave to ENGLAND today. Lt. R.A. WALKER is in temporary Command.	N.S.D
July 22nd	Effective Strength of this Unit is now 14-46 01 or LT. R.A. WALKER having been absorbed in the establishment of this Unit. The weather today is good and the ground is in good condition.	N.S.D
July 23rd	Inter Section relief took place today. 8pm 'B' Section L/F SAINS EN GOHELLE and proceeded to the line to relieve 'A' Section, who, on relief	

Army Form C. 2118.

WAR DIARY JULY 1918
or
INTELLIGENCE SUMMARY.
(Erase heading not required.)

Instructions regarding War Diaries and Intelligence Summaries are contained in F. S. Regs., Part II. and the Staff Manual respectively. Title pages will be prepared in manuscript.

Hour, Date, Place	Summary of Events and Information	Remarks and references to Appendices
July 23". 2.a.m	Marched to its rest billets.	H.S.D.
July 25. COMBAT.T.R.	The gun in position here fired 84 rounds at ranges from 500 to 800 yards on targets arranged with the 9th EAST SURREY REGT, in a preliminary bout.	
	Advanced for a raid.	H.S.D.
CUTOFF.	This gun, at 700 yards range fired 74 rounds.	
July 26".	2.O.R. were struck off the strength of this unit, and application was made for 2 to replace them.	H.S.D.
July 27".	2 LT E.G. IBBS. E.R. W KENT REGT was struck off the establishment on notification being received of his transfer to ENGLAND. An application was formally made for 2LT C.L. REID 1st N STAFFS REGT to be posted to complete	H.S.D.

Forms/C. 2118/11.

WAR DIARY or INTELLIGENCE SUMMARY

JULY 1918

Army Form C. 2118.

Hour, Date, Place	Summary of Events and Information	Remarks and references to Appendices
July 27 (Cont.)	Establishment.	JAD
July 28.	Weather continues wet & showery, which however has not much effect on the roads, as the chalk allows rain to filter through.	JAD
July 29.	All guns in reserve positions were ranged with undetonated ammunition which was afterwards salved. The guns were then tested for extreme range.	JAD
July 30th	The weather today was fine, slight mists prevailing towards evening.	JAD
July 31st	The climatic conditions today were excellent.	JAD

W.S. Drewke Capt.
For O/C 72 L. A.A.- Bty

Confidential

War Diary

1st Brig. French Mortar Battery

1st. August to 31st. August 1918.

Volume IV

Army Form C. 2118.

WAR DIARY
or
INTELLIGENCE SUMMARY.
(Erase heading not required.)

AUGUST 1918.

Instructions regarding War Diaries and Intelligence Summaries are contained in F. S. Regs., Part II. and the Staff Manual respectively. Title pages will be prepared in manuscript.

Hour, Date, Place	Summary of Events and Information	Remarks and references to Appendices
Aug 1st – 2nd 1918	The weather for this period was extremely wet, rain falling continually.	WSD
Aug 4th	There is a great improvement in the weather, the roads are rapidly drying. Inter Sec: relief was carried out, B Section relieving 'A' in the line.	
7.30 pm	'B' Section under 2/Lt C.L. Reid, left its rest billets in SAINS-EN-GOHELLE and proceeded to the line.	
12.15 a.m.	Relief was completed, 'A' Section, under 2/Lt A.C. Nilson marched to, and took over its rest billets.	WSD
Aug 5th & 6th	The weather these two days was dull and cold. Rain also fell and mist was also present. Considerable activity is reported from the 2 retaliatory guns in action, firing being chiefly confined to daytime on account	WSD

Army Form C. 2118.

WAR DIARY for August 1915
or
INTELLIGENCE SUMMARY.
(Erase heading not required.)

Instructions regarding War Diaries and Intelligence Summaries are contained in F. S. Regs., Part II. and the Staff Manual respectively. Title pages will be prepared in manuscript.

Hour, Date, Place	Summary of Events and Information	Remarks and references to Appendices
	Sanction was obtained for 1 Gun to be taken out of the line for instructional purposes. In case of an order "Prepare for action", the gun must invariably be kept in readiness to be taken up the line, and on the receipt of that order, to be put in position. No 1 Gun was accordingly sent out of the line. The gun in COMBAT fired 59 rounds on Enemy sap opposite MASONS HOUSE.	W.S.B.
Aug 7 & 8	The weather for this period was fine. 2 Guns fired 48 rounds, engaging various targets as released by the infantry. CAPT H.S. DAINTREE M.C. relieved LT. R.A. WALKER at the Tet. Ars; the last named officer proceed on leave to U.K. Hostile artillery was quiet, except for slight	

Army Form C. 2118.

WAR DIARY for August 1918.
or
INTELLIGENCE SUMMARY.
(Erase heading not required.)

Hour, Date, Place	Summary of Events and Information	Remarks and references to Appendices
	Our patrols out during the night. The trenches in this sector, although muddy, are not as bad as one would expect. This is largely on account of the light nature of the soil which allows to a very large extent, the rain to filter through. Hostile artillery was very active, maintaining a heavy bombardment on the reserve positions up to 5 p.m., with shells of all calibres. Several shells fell near Bty HQrs but no direct hits were obtained. The front line was quiet. Trench Mortar Bombs, believed to be Medium, were reported as falling short near MASON'S HOUSE. These, however, were probably our own bombs, as orders had been issued to the CUT OFF GUN to fire on an enemy M.G. position opposite MASON'S HOUSE during the night.	MSP
6 Aug. 7 Aug.	The night was quiet, rain falling in showers. The BGC's	

IV

Army Form C. 2118.

Instructions regarding War Diaries and Intelligence
Summaries are contained in F. S. Regs., Part II.
and the Staff Manual respectively. Title pages
will be prepared in manuscript.

WAR DIARY for August 1915
or
INTELLIGENCE SUMMARY.
(Erase heading not required.)

Hour, Date, Place	Summary of Events and Information	Remarks and references to Appendices
	activity during the night. Effective strength of this Unit at present 4 off - 46 O.R	MD
Aug 9	The weather today was good. Hostile artillery which was rather active on OPERA - HOUSE and FOSSE 16, was neutralised by our artillery. Enemy bombing in the rear areas has become considerable during the nights.	MD
Aug 10 & 11	All blue rings were removed from shells in Reserve gun pits. Two mules of this unit were killed by an enemy bomb during the night. Our attached strength is now 2 I.O.R. and 6, instead of 8 mules	
Aug 12	The weather for this period was very good. Inter Section relief was carried out. 'A' Section	

(9 29 6) W 2794 100,000 5/14 H W V   Forms/C. 2118/11.

Army Form C. 2118.

WAR DIARY for August 1915
or
INTELLIGENCE SUMMARY.
(Erase heading not required.)

Hour, Date, Place	Summary of Events and Information	Remarks and references to Appendices
	Under LT. A.C. NILSON relieving B. Section in the line.	ALB.
Aug 12.	The usual retaliatory firing from the 2 guns was carried out. This was chiefly in answer to Enemy aerial darts, which displayed great activity.	ALB.
Aug 13ᵃ - 16.	The weather for this period was very hot. Many casualties among civilians are reported, caused by enemy bombs. As a precaution the rest billets of the Bty have been made as scattered as possible. Houses are occupied and affording no protection, leaving all details in our house, as heretofore, would be extremely dangerous.	ALB.
Aug 16.	CAPT. H. S. DAINTREE M.C. proceeded to 46 Divne Sig to attend conference + demonstration on organization + forming of platoons by Inspector General	

Forms/C. 2118/11

WAR DIARY for August 1915
or
INTELLIGENCE SUMMARY.
(Erase heading not required.)

Army Form C. 2118.

Hour, Date, Place	Summary of Events and Information	Remarks and references to Appendices
7.15 pm	of Infantry Training. 'B' Section under 2Lt. C. L. REID left its tents for the line to relieve 'A' Section	MSR
10.15 pm	Relief was duly completed.	MSR
Aug 19	Effectives strength of this Unit is now 4 Off. 45 O.R., 1 O.R. being struck off on account of evacuation to No 33 C.C.S. Guns Nos 3 & 4 moved into new positions at M.18.c.15.60.	
6 pm	This operation was duly completed.	

Army Form C. 2118.

WAR DIARY /or August 1916

INTELLIGENCE SUMMARY.

(Erase heading not required.)

Instructions regarding War Diaries and Intelligence Summaries are contained in F. S. Regs., Part II. and the Staff Manual respectively. Title pages will be prepared in manuscript.

Hour, Date, Place	Summary of Events and Information	Remarks and references to Appendices
Aug 20th	The weather still continues fine, prevalent wind being from the west.	HB
Aug 22nd	Our back areas were persistently shelled by enemy long range guns of large calibre throughout the day.	HB
Aug 23rd	Inter sector relief was carried out. A Sector relieving B in the line. The relief B Sector made 24th REID proceeded to SAINS EN GOHELLE to occupy its rest billets.	HB
Aug 24th – 27th	The weather for this period was good. On account of enemy shelling, preparations are being made for all units to leave SAINS EN GOHELLE as it is thought that the shelling is on account of	

VIII

Army Form C. 2118.

WAR DIARY for Aug 1918.
or
INTELLIGENCE SUMMARY.
(Erase heading not required.)

Instructions regarding War Diaries and Intelligence
Summaries are contained in F. S. Regs., Part II.
and the Staff Manual respectively. Title pages
will be prepared in manuscript.

Hour, Date, Place	Summary of Events and Information	Remarks and references to Appendices
	Units Transport Lines being located in the village.	
	Effective strength of this Unit is now 3off - 46 O.R.	
	1.O.R was today struck off and 1.O.R posted to complete the establishment.	JRR
Aug 28th	Rain which fell throughout the day led to effect on the moral which were greatly dried by a strong sun. Inter Section relief was today carried out 'B' relieving 'A' Section in the Line on relief 'A' Section proceeded to SAINS-EN-GOHELLE, as permission has been obtained for this Unit to retain its rest billets there.	JRR
Aug 29th - 31st	The weather conditions for this period were extremely good.	

W.S. Downton Capt.
For O/C 76th Trench Mortar Battery

(9 29 6) W 2791 100,000 8/14 H W V Forms/C. 2118/11.

Secret.

War Diary
of
72nd T.M. Batty.
September 1918

Army Form C. 2118.

WAR DIARY for Sept 1918.
or
INTELLIGENCE SUMMARY.
(Erase heading not required.)

Hour, Date, Place	Summary of Events and Information	Remarks and references to Appendices
Sept 1. 1918	Notification was received that the enemy had evacuated LENS on the night 31 Aug/1st Sept and had established himself on the OPPY-MERICOURT-VENDIN Line. Orders were immediately issued to the Gun Teams, all firing was to cease on account of patrol activity in day time. The teams stood by awaiting orders from the O.C. on application of the Battalion Commander for guns to destroy hostile T.M. and M.G. Emplacements. The weather conditions today were good, the ground being in a hard condition.	W.89.
Sept 2"	Ammunition was prepared at the Dumps to be carried to the Guns when necessary. Up to 11.a.m. no firing was done.	

Army Form C. 2118.

WAR DIARY Sept 1915.
or
INTELLIGENCE SUMMARY.
(Erase heading not required.)

Hour, Date, Place	Summary of Events and Information	Remarks and references to Appendices
Sept 2 (cont). 11 p.m.	A message was received concerning hostile M.G. firing from N.14.6.40.65 (LENS SHT 4+A). A gun team was duly warned to take its gun forward and engage this target. The Company Commander concerned, however, decided not to fire. The weather today was dull during the morning, but considerably cleaner during the evening.	W.S.D.
Sept 3rd	Infantry carrying parties for ammunition were arranged. Inter Section relief was today carried out. 'B' relieving 'D' Section in the line.	
10.30 pm.	On completion of relief 'B' Section under LT REID proceeded to SAINS EN GOHELLE to occupy its rest billets	

Army Form C. 2118.

WAR DIARY Sept 1915
or
INTELLIGENCE SUMMARY.
(Erase heading not required.)

Hour, Date, Place	Summary of Events and Information	Remarks and references to Appendices
Sept 3rd	Weather conditions today were good.	W.S.D.
Sept 4th	On night 3/4th the gun in position at N.8.C.70.05 fired 95 rounds on target at N.8.0.80.20. During the daytime the gun is withdrawn to N.8.C.30.70.	
9 pm.	Two guns were placed in positions at N.8.C.70.05 and 200 rounds of ammunition was stocked there by infantry carrying parties. Two guns were also placed at N.13.d.95.10. The weather during day was good. During the night the wind was slightly in enemy's favour. Slight rain also fell.	
Sept 5th	The gun in position at N.8.C.70.05 fired 106 rounds and withdrew to its rear position where it remained until dusk. A decision was made.	W.S.D.

WAR DIARY Sept 19.15
or
INTELLIGENCE SUMMARY.
(Erase heading not required.)

Army Form C. 2118.

How, Date, Place	Summary of Events and Information	Remarks and references to Appendices
	to put 2 guns in position at N.8.c.30.65. An infantry carrying party reporting was sent with 120 rounds to this position. In order to ensure swift retaliation our gun position at N.13.d.90.15 is fitted with a telephone. A cellar in the vicinity of this position is being transformed into an ammunition store and gun emplacement. An alternate position here has been chosen by the O.C., which is also being developed and stocked with 300 rounds of ammunition. All ammunition sent to the forward guns is invariably cleaned and thoroughly examined by members of the rear gun teams. A mist prevailed today from 5am to 10am. The weather for the remainder of the day was fine, with a slight wind.	

WAR DIARY Sept 1918
or
INTELLIGENCE SUMMARY.
(Erase heading not required.)

Army Form C. 2118.

Hour, Date, Place	Summary of Events and Information	Remarks and references to Appendices
Sept 6"	60 rounds were fired by the gun in position at N.8.C.70.05 as required by the 6.6 forward Coy. Work is proceeding on cellar and trench at N13.d.90.15. The weather today was fair until the afternoon when rain fell and later a heavy thunderstorm took place.	W.D.
Sept 7"	In accordance with a Brigade scheme to form an advanced dump for Stokes Shells a pillbox at N12.6.30.70 is being prepared by members of the reserve gun teams. An infantry carrying party today carried 400 rounds to this form this reserve. The weather today was very dull and wet and a heavy storm took place during the afternoon.	W.D.

WAR DIARY
or
INTELLIGENCE SUMMARY.
(Erase heading not required.)

Army Form C. 2118.

Sept 1918

Hour, Date, Place	Summary of Events and Information	Remarks and references to Appendices
Sept 9th	Inter section relief today took place, 'B' relieving 'A' Section in the line. Leaving SAINS EN GOHELLE at 6.30 p.m, B Section proceeded to the line, and relieved 'A' Section by 10.45 p.m. 'A' Section on relief proceeded to the rest billets vacated by 'B'. The weather today was dull, rain fell throughout the day. The prevalent wind was of a westerly direction, a slight mist also prevailed.	W.S.D.
Sept 10th.	Drizzling rain fell throughout the day.	W.S.D.
Sept 11th.	The weather conditions today were good.	W.S.D.
Sept 12th. 8-10 p.m.	During the morning the weather was good, but in the afternoon and evening rain fell. To ensure swift retaliation a full set toad arr-	

Army Form C. 2118.

WAR DIARY Sept 1918
or
INTELLIGENCE SUMMARY.
(Erase heading not required.)

Instructions regarding War Diaries and Intelligence Summaries are contained in F. S. Regs., Part II. and the Staff Manual respectively. Title pages will be prepared in manuscript.

Place	Date	Hour	Summary of Events and Information	Remarks and references to Appendices
			anger from a forward post to our gun in CONDUCTOR. Thus in the event of a hostile raid the gun team would be immediately warned and therefore swift action would be assured. Retaliatory firing has now ceased. Guns fire only in the event of hostile raids in the vicinity of their targets, or by special request of the infantry.	A.D.
	13/9/18.		The trenches in this sector are, for the most part, in a bad condition, on account of the spell of wet weather. Rain fell today.	A.D.
	14/9/18.		The enemy attempted a raid on one of our forward posts at our gun in CONDUCTOR ALLEY was, however apprised of this, and in the prompt action which followed was the means of a repulse.	A.D.
	15/9/18		Today the weather conditions were excellent, in spite of a slight mist prevalent.	A.D.

Army Form C. 2118.

Instructions regarding War Diaries and Intelligence
Summaries are contained in F. S. Regs., Part II.
and the Staff Manual respectively. Title pages
will be prepared in manuscript.

WAR DIARY Sept 19/5
or
INTELLIGENCE SUMMARY.
(Erase heading not required.)

Hour, Date, Place	Summary of Events and Information	Remarks and references to Appendices
Sept 15th	2 gun positions were today handed over to the "B". French Mortar Battery. Inter Section relief being in operation today. "A" Section relieves "B" in the line.	
11.15 p.m.	On relief completed "B" Section under 2 Lt. C.L. REID proceeded to SAINS EN GOHELLE, to occupy the rest billets.	
Sept 16th	2 gun positions were taken over from the 17th French Mortar Battery, but of these 2 only were occupied by this unit. All guns are situated in the open but cellars in close proximity afford accommodation for the gun teams. One sap is also occupied.	
Sept 17th	The weather today was good, although dull during the morning.	

IX

Army Form C. 2118.

Instructions regarding War Diaries and Intelligence
Summaries are contained in F. S. Regs., Part II.
and the Staff Manual respectively. Title pages
will be prepared in manuscript.

WAR DIARY Sept 1916.
or
INTELLIGENCE SUMMARY.
(Erase heading not required.)

Hour, Date, Place	Summary of Events and Information	Remarks and references to Appendices
Sept 18th	The weather today was good although observation was poor.	N.S.D.
Sept 19th	The O.C. ordered a Conference of Officers which assembled at the Rear Headquarters at 4.30 p.m. The object in view was to discuss various problems. The chief point of discussion was the action of this Unit in case of an enemy withdrawal. All arrangements regarding the supply of rations and ammunition have been settled. The weather today was good.	N.S.D.
Sept 20th	Today's weather was wet. The wind, being slightly in enemy's favour during the night, gas sentries were on the alert.	N.S.D.
Sept 21st	The weather today was good.	

(3 29 6) W 2791 100,000 8/14 H W V   Forms/C. 2118/11.

WAR DIARY
or
INTELLIGENCE SUMMARY.
(Erase heading not required.)

Sept 1915.

Army Form C. 2118.

Hour, Date, Place	Summary of Events and Information	Remarks and references to Appendices
Sept 21st	(cont). "B" Section relieved "A" Section in the line. Leaving SAINS EN GOHELLE at 6:30 pm 'B' Section under 2LT C.L REID proceeded to the line and relieved 'A' who on relief under LT.R.A. WALKER marched and took over the rest billets evacuated by 'B'.	H.S.D.
Sept 22.	The Enemy inconsistently shelled our reserve positions throughout the day. Towards the evening hostile artillery was, however, neutralized by our own artillery. The weather was today good but observation was poor. The establishment of this Unit is now complete ie 4 officers - 46 other ranks. In addition to this 19 O.R are attached, remaining on the strength of their Battalions but doing duty with this Unit.	W.B.
Sept 23. 8pm.	One gun cooperated in a raid with the 8th R.W KENT RGT.	

Army Form C. 2118.

WAR DIARY Sept 1915.
or
INTELLIGENCE SUMMARY.
(Erase heading not required.)

Instructions regarding War Diaries and Intelligence Summaries are contained in F. S. Regs., Part II. and the Staff Manual respectively. Title pages will be prepared in manuscript.

Hour, Date, Place		Summary of Events and Information	Remarks and references to Appendices
Sept 23	8pm.	(Cont) Under previous arrangement one gun moved forward and fired 20 rounds, employing a range of 650 yards. According to the programme 3 and rounds were then expended, as the raiding party on reaching their objective would incur great risk through the use of live rounds.	R.D.
Sept 25"		Throughout the day a singling rain fell. The O.C. attended a conference at Advanced H.A.: aw 72. I. B. A notification was received of a purposed raid on the enemy trenches on the 26" inst. An infantry carrying party for ammunition was immediately called for.	R.D.
Sept 26"	3pm.	Three guns of this Unit cooperated in a raid with the 8th R.W.KENT RGT. At 3pm fire was opened at ranges varying from 450 - 600 yards. The targets	

Army Form C. 2118.

WAR DIARY Sept. 1916
or
INTELLIGENCE SUMMARY.
(Erase heading not required.)

Place	Date	Hour	Summary of Events and Information	Remarks and references to Appendices
	26/9/16 (Cont).		Chiefly trench junctions. 284 rounds were expended with excellent results. Arrangements were made for the teams of all forward guns to be withdrawn to a safe in rear, on account of a heavy bombardment of enemy positions on the morning of the 27th, when great hostile retaliation was anticipated.	HQ.
	27/9/16.		A working party of the resting section proceeded to the line for the purpose of cleaning ammunition preparatory to handing over to the incoming division. An advance party of 173" 2" M.B. was met at BULLY GRENAY and conducted to the line.	HQ.
	28/9/16.		The Battery was relieved in the line by the 173rd Trench Mortar Battery, incoming gun teams being conducted to the line by a guide from our H.Qrs. All guns were exchanged, complete with the exception of tool bags and cleaning rods.	
	29/9/16. 11. p.m.		Relief was completed. On relief 'B' Section proceeded to BULLY GRENAY, where they were met by lorries and conveyed to HERSIN, where they joined 'A' Section who had proceeded from SAINS-EN-GOHELLE at 1.p.m. Huts are occupied by all O.Rs, the officers being established in private billets.	

XIII.

WAR DIARY Sept 1918.
or
INTELLIGENCE SUMMARY.
Army Form C. 2118.

Place	Date	Hour	Summary of Events and Information	Remarks and references to Appendices
	29/9/18	(cont).	The establishment of this Unit was reduced to 4 offr - 45 O.R on account of 1 O.R being transferred to the 25th Div. L 2 m Bties. Weather Conditions were today very bad.	HKB
	30/9/18		At 9.a.m the Battery paraded in full marching order, under the O.C and proceeded to COUPIGNY - HERSIN Station from where entrainment was made, and the destination, BOUQUE MAISON reached at 4-45 pm. Here the men's forces were transferred to a motor lorry as an extremely long march was anticipated. An advance party consisting of 1 officer, 1 O.R had previously proceeded on to the resting area to arrange billets. The Battery less a few O.R's who were conveyed by lorry marched to WARLUZEL, arriving there at 8 p.m, when the arranged billets were occupied. Officers are established in a private house and O R S in barns.	

H.S. Bainbridge Capt
O.C. 72nd Trench Mortar Battery.

CONFIDENTIAL

WAR DIARY
of
72ⁿᵈ Light Trench Mortar Batty.
OCTOBER 1918

WAR DIARY
or
INTELLIGENCE SUMMARY.
(Erase heading not required.)

October 1918.

Army Form C. 2118.

Hour, Date, Place	Summary of Events and Information	Remarks and references to Appendices
Oct. 1st	In accordance with a Training Programme which had been drawn up, various exercises were carried out. Special emphasis is laid on Athletic pursuits.	H.S.D.
Oct 2nd	Experiments were carried out regarding the use of steel hats in place of helmets during active operations. As this type of warfare is to be expected in future all unnecessary weight has to be cut down in view of portability. It was thought that if well members of the gun team carried I spare steel hat, not only would minimum weight be carried, but that the gun crew thereby be brought into action in the minimum of time. This latter fact is perhaps the more important of the two as it will be seen that during an advance the necessity for quick action is imperative. The results of the Experiments	

WAR DIARY
or
INTELLIGENCE SUMMARY.

(Erase heading not required.)

Army Form C. 2118.

October 1918.

Hour, Date, Place	Summary of Events and Information	Remarks and references to Appendices
	were satisfactory. It was found that when firing from hand, bursts such as a rate as many as five rounds could be fired from the same hat. The advisability of discarding the gun mountings was also considered. A type of handle for the gun pose of firing without a mounting is available. Experiments on these also proven satisfactory.	H.S.P.
Oct 3"	The Battery participated in a Tactical Scheme etc 12th Infantry Brigade. Two guns and gun teams, each under the Command of an Officer worked in conjunction with each Battalion. Firing was done by means of Skid hats and handles.	H.S.P.
Oct 4"	The usual training programme was carried out.	

Army Form C. 2118.

WAR DIARY October 1918
or
INTELLIGENCE SUMMARY.
(Erase heading not required.)

Instructions regarding War Diaries and Intelligence Summaries are contained in F.S. Regs., Part II. and the Staff Manual respectively. Title pages will be prepared in manuscript.

Hour, Date, Place		Summary of Events and Information	Remarks and references to Appendices
Oct 5th	9.30 a.m.	The Bty paraded, and under the O.C. marched to MONTÉCOURT, where Entrainment was made.	
	6.30 pm	Detrainment was made at FREMICOURT where, a guide from the advance party was waiting, who conducted the Bty to GRAINCOURT. Accommodation was provided by bivouacs situated in open country.	ASD.
Oct 6th		12. O.R. were sent to join the Divisional Wing, this being the surplus personnel, which in accordance with a Divisional Order had to comprise 25% of the personnel of all Units. The remainder of the Bty, having been duly warned for gun teams proceeded under Lt. R.A. WALKER to CANTAING. Here cellars were provided as billets. From there the nearer teams under the Sgt Major moved to a forward ammunition dump, which had been	

Forms/C. 2118/11.

Army Form C. 2118.

WAR DIARY October 1918
or
INTELLIGENCE SUMMARY.
(Erase heading not required.)

Hour, Date, Place	Summary of Events and Information	Remarks and references to Appendices
	Selected Ammunition was then carried by the reserve teams and stored at the dumps. This ammunition was then cleaned, detonators and cartridges and packed, in readiness for the various carrying parties which duly arrived with the 6 remaining teams.	
	Each group of 2 guns, with carrying party on being supplied with ammunition moved forward and attached themselves to their respective Battalions. Positions were taken up in rear of the infantry, and firing was at the discretion of the Company Commander. From then, and throughout action in conjunction with Kent Battalion, Rations were supplied by this Unit and, to avoid inconvenience and delay, they were delivered by each Battalion.	W.S./

Army Form C. 2118.

WAR DIARY October 1918.
or
INTELLIGENCE SUMMARY.
(Erase heading not required.)

Hour, Date, Place	Summary of Events and Information	Remarks and references to Appendices
Oct 17th 1918.	Inter Divisional relief took place, the 19th relieving the 2nd Division. As each gun team was released in proceeded to Rear HQrs where they were all collected. As advance party proceeded to CAMBRAI amongst billets.	W.S.P.
Oct 18th	The Bty under the O.C. marched to CAMBRAI and were Here met by the Advance Party and conducted to its billets. Two houses were occupied, the Bty being accommodated in the larger house and the Officers in the smaller one.	W.S.P.
Oct 19th & 20th.	These days were spent in cleaning up the guns, equipments &c	W.S.P.
Oct 21st	A request for reinforcements which had been based on the 19th brought the following reinforcements to the Unit. 9 E Surrey Regt - 2.O.R. 6th R.W.Kents - 3.O.R. 1 N.Staffs.Regt. - 6.O.R. The training programme which had been previously arr-	

Army Form C. 2118.

WAR DIARY
or
INTELLIGENCE SUMMARY.
(Erase heading not required.)

October 1916

Instructions regarding War Diaries and Intelligence
Summaries are contained in F. S. Regs., Part II.
and the Staff Manual respectively. Title pages
will be prepared in manuscript.

Hour, Date, Place	Summary of Events and Information	Remarks and references to Appendices
Oct 22	Anzac was carried out.	WSP.
Oct 23	Weather conditions were favourable to the execution of the Training Programme. Special Emphasis is being laid on athletic pursuits.	WSP.
Oct 24	2 Enemy Light MinenWerfer Guns were relieved by the O.C. A great many rounds were also asked. Experiments were carried out with the MinenWerfer Gun. These were entirely successful. 10th, 2Lt. P.C. BRUNGER, E.Rn KENT R.Gt reported for duty with this Unit.	WSP. HR.
Oct 25	The Bty participated in a Tactical Scheme with the Brigade. Two guns and teams were detailed for	

Forms/C. 2118/11

WAR DIARY
or
INTELLIGENCE SUMMARY.
(Erase heading not required.)

Army Form C. 2118.

October 1918.

Hour, Date, Place	Summary of Events and Information	Remarks and references to Appendices
	duty with each Battalion.	
Oct 27. Jan.	The Btty paraded under the O.C and marched with the Brigade to AVESNES-LES-AUBERT. The advance party had previously arranged for three houses to be used as billets. These were accordingly occupied. 2 Enemy L.T.M's were also brought.	1112 M.D.
Oct 28 - 31.	The weather conditions were extremely favourable. The guns were employed for a practice of street fighting and ranges were taken to supposed M.G. positions, with a view to their destruction if in actual warfare. Demonstrations were given on the light Minenwerfer guns to officers of the Brigade.	K.S

W.S. Dawtra Capt
O/C Trench Mortar Battery.

Appendix I.

Date, hour, Place.	Summary of Events
Period 7-15th Octr.	The weather for this period was on the whole fine and suitable for the operations such as were carried out. Rain fell at intervals but not in sufficient quantities so to hamper the progress of our troops. With the Stokes Guns, although great difficulty was experienced getting the guns into action, greater difficulty was experienced in keeping the ammunition dry. 1 Limber and team of mules was stationed at Rear H.Qrs for the purpose of bringing up ammunition which was so made into dumps at various places in rear of the guns. As the ammunition was required by the gun groups it was conveyed by means of a carrying party, one of which was provided by each of the respective Battalions. For this period all firing was done with steel retainers, and handles All baseplates and mountings were, however, carried by the B Echelon of the Transport, so that, in the event of their being required they were available.

Date	hour - place	Summary of Events.
Oct 11th		LT. R.A. WALKER, 8 R.W.KENT.RGT was admitted to Hospital sick. As this left 2 Officers only for duty with the guns this place was taken by the Sergt Major. 1.O.R was wounded.
Oct 15th		An order reached 'B' Echelon of the Transport that baseplates were required. These were accordingly conveyed to Head Quarters. 2.O.R were wounded.
Oct 16th	5.30am HAUSSY	An attack was made by the Brigade. All objectives and the village of HAUSSY was gained. At night, however, the enemy counter attacked in force, and although the left flank held on, the right gave way. In attacking the village, the river SELLE had to be crossed. This was done by means of bridges thrown across by the R.E.s. By the counter attack the Enemy regained possession of the village as far as the river. Expended 60 rounds — Dir The guns acting with the 8th Q. W. Kent Rgt. firing from the canal

Date, hour, Place.	Summary of Events.
	one round, silenced an enemy machine gun which was holding up the troops. On account of the damp fuzes, however, all attempts at firing were given up. The teams with the 9th East Surrey Regt got into position in a sunken road and fired vigorously when the enemy's counter attack, however forced the regiment to relinquish the village and the 2 guns were left in the hands of the enemy. 2 LT. A.C. NILSON, 9th E SURREY. RGT and 5. O.R were missing. The weather was very wet. W.S. Dainties Capt

72nd T.M. Battery.

WAR DIARY
or
INTELLIGENCE SUMMARY.
(Erase heading not required.)

Army Form C. 2118.

December, 1918.

Hour, Date, Place	Summary of Events and Information	Remarks and references to Appendices
1st December to 12th Dec.	Battery quartered at CARNOY FARM NOMAIN, engaged in Gun Drill, Infantry Drill, P.T. and recreational training	
13th December, 1918	Battery moved with other Brigade units to TOURNAI	
19th December 1918 – 31st December 1918.	Battery quartered in l'Ecole Normale, Rue CLOQUEDENT, TOURNAI. For the first few days all ranks were engaged in cleaning and improving billets and therefter drill and P.T. were carried out daily until on 30th December Educational classes were begun under the instructorship of officers and N.C.Os. The classes included French, Arithmetic, English, Map Reading and the men generally showed good promise of much improvement after a few weeks had elapsed.	C.L. Nead 2/L OC 72nd T.M.B

72nd Jewish Infantry Battalion

WAR DIARY
INTELLIGENCE SUMMARY
(Erase heading not required.)

Army Form C. 2118.

Hour, Date, Place	Summary of Events and Information	Remarks and references to Appendices
January 1st to 15th	From 1st of January to the 15th the Battn. was occupied with several Tasks; and in the short time available (09.30 to 12.30 Rms. each day) considerable progress was made by all in the following subjects:— English, Arithmetic, French and Scotland; three lines devoted by Sergeant Instrs on special subjects; "What we owe to the Navy" given by 2/Lt P.C. Bruayn; two very well prepared, a very interesting and instructive talk was given by S.E. Battn. on its daily doings; Topic of the Government Scheme for Repatriating work on the land; Each of the different officers of the Battn gave an instruction in his own subject and actions, assisted by 2/Lt Byrne (French and Arithmetic) and thereunon Alphonse Rabie (French), who very kindly lent his services for an occasional hour or two each week. Short, elementary and advanced classes were held in those subjects. This was especially desirable in the case of English (Composition, Dictation, and Letter-writing — all pupils and advanced) and Arithmetic, on naturally some of the men were more advanced than others.	

72nd Trench Mortar Battery

Army Form C. 2118.

WAR DIARY
or
INTELLIGENCE SUMMARY.
(Erase heading not required.)

Hour, Date, Place	Summary of Events and Information	Remarks and references to Appendices
1919 January 1st to 15th (Cntd)	A very gratifying result of a fortnight's tuition by Sgt Jurd is that two men, who previously were unable to either read or write, can now print themselves on being able to both lonely well. They are not, at present, hands to do this tuition on the strictest sense of the lesson, and, with practice, will mend highly. At first, the men considered the educational scheme a "waste of time"; but as they found themselves progressing, their keenness grew. It is very gratifying to note that the men were never disinclined to the voluntary work in this part. They are too keen on any alternative to miserable squander-lands at present. Then physical bathes are not lost sight of, but each morning they were taken for full an hour in organised games and physical training. The afternoons were generally given over to athletic and recreational pursuits. The matches played between the 72nd J.M.B. and other teams were keenly followed by the rest of the Battery. Note: our team was amalgamated with the Brigade Headquarters	

72nd Trench Mortar Battery

Army Form C. 2118.

WAR DIARY
or
INTELLIGENCE SUMMARY.
(Erase heading not required.)

Instructions regarding War Diaries and Intelligence Summaries are contained in F. S. Regs., Part II. and the Staff Manual respectively. Title pages will be prepared in manuscript.

Hour, Date, Place	Summary of Events and Information	Remarks and references to Appendices
January 15th to 31st.	Football (Soccer) Team. On an average a very successful return drive was held in the town Tesa-room.	GP/
	From 15th January until the end of the month all available men of the Battery have been working daily at the Divisional Ammunition Dump at the LEUZE Road. This the ammunition return has been brought to a standstill — for the time being, in despite.	
	During the period available reserves, the men of the Battery have been comfortably billeted in the back streets, and generally speaking they have been very contented and cheerful.	
	On the month of January ten (10) men of the Battery were demobilised.	GP.

N.S. Dunbar Capt.
O.C. 72nd T.M.B.

www.ingramcontent.com/pod-product-compliance
Lightning Source LLC
Chambersburg PA
CBHW081451160426
43193CB00013B/2442